THE STUDENT'S GUIDE TO WRITING

THE STUDENT'S GUIDE TO WRITING

Essential Outlines and Strategies

DR. PUNTWIDA L. TREZVANT

To order additional copies of this book, contact:
Xlibris
844-714-8691
www.Xlibris.com
Orders@Xlibris.com
866300

DEDICATION

To my daughter, Amia, whose unwavering love and support continue to inspire me every day.

To my granddog, Dolce, for the joy, laughter, and emotional support you bring into my life.

To my parents, Michael Sr. and Linda J., whose guidance and encouragement shaped me into the person I am today.

To my brother, Michael Jr., his fiancée, Tamia, and my nephews, Michael, Malachi, Matthew, Moses, my niece, Mariah, and my great-nephew, Michael Lee, for the love, laughter, and strength you all bring into my life.

And to all my students—past, present, and future—whose dedication, challenges, and growth inspired me to write this book. Your journey is the reason this work exists.

This book is for all of you, with love and gratitude.

Thank you **God** for everything!

CONTENTS

CONTENTS

CHAPTER ONE

THE WRITING PROCESS

1. Prewriting (Planning)

This is the phase where you lay the foundation for your writing.

- **Brainstorming**: Generate ideas, either through freewriting, mind mapping, or listing.
- **Research**: If necessary, gather information, sources, or references to support your writing.
- **Audience and Purpose**: Consider who will be reading your work and why you are writing it. This will help shape the tone, style, and content.
- **Outlining**: Organize your ideas into a structure (e.g., a traditional outline with main points and subpoints, or a visual map). This will help you know what to write and in what order.

2. Drafting

In this stage, you begin writing the actual content. The goal is to get your ideas down on paper (or screen), without worrying too much about perfection.

- **Write the first draft**: Focus on getting the ideas across, rather than on making it perfect. It's okay if the sentences are rough.
- **Follow your outline**: Use it as a guide, but feel free to adapt if your ideas evolve as you write.
- **Keep the flow going**: Don't get bogged down in editing during this phase. Just focus on making progress.

3. Revising

This is the stage where you refine your ideas and improve the overall structure and flow of your writing.

- **Evaluate content**: Look at the overall structure. Are your ideas clear? Is there a logical flow between paragraphs?
- **Develop ideas**: Flesh out any sections that may feel underdeveloped. Add examples, explanations, or details where necessary.
- **Rearrange sections**: If needed, reorder paragraphs or sentences to improve the clarity and impact of your writing.
- **Check tone and style**: Ensure that the tone is appropriate for your audience and purpose.

4. Editing

In this stage, you focus on improving the quality of the writing at the sentence level.

- **Grammar and punctuation**: Correct any mistakes with grammar, punctuation, spelling, and sentence structure.
- **Clarity and conciseness**: Ensure each sentence is clear and to the point. Eliminate wordiness and repetition.
- **Sentence flow**: Make sure sentences are varied in structure and length, and that they flow smoothly together.
- **Check for consistency**: Ensure consistent use of tenses, voice, and terminology.

5. Proofreading

This is the final step before submitting or publishing your work, where you focus on small details.

- **Check for typos**: Look for spelling errors, missing words, or repeated words.
- **Check formatting**: Ensure that the document follows the proper format (e.g., font, margins, spacing) and citation style (if applicable).
- **Final review**: Read the text one last time, preferably out loud, to catch any last-minute mistakes or awkward phrasing.

6. Publishing/Submission

After proofreading, your writing is ready for its intended audience.

- **Submit or share**: Depending on your purpose, this might mean submitting your work for a class, sending it to an editor, publishing it online, or printing it out.
- **Reflection**: After publishing, reflect on the process. What worked well? What could be improved for next time?

Note: Formal writing is professional, structured, and uses proper grammar, avoiding slang or contractions. It's used in academic, business, or official contexts. Informal writing is casual, conversational, and may include contractions, slang, and a more relaxed tone, commonly used in personal communication or creative works.

CHAPTER TWO

DISCUSSION BOARD OUTLINES AND REPLIES

Introduction:

In online learning environments, discussion boards are vital for fostering communication and critical thinking among students. Crafting an effective discussion board outline allows you to organize your thoughts clearly and engage with the material in a structured manner. In this chapter, we'll explore the steps necessary to create a well-organized discussion post and reply. You'll learn how to structure your initial post to present your ideas effectively, as well as how to reply thoughtfully to your peers, providing valuable feedback and insight. Refer to the examples provided to better understand how to construct meaningful discussion board posts and replies.

Note: Your initial discussion board post should typically be 250–300 words, unless your instructor provides different guidelines. A strong post includes an introduction to introduce your topic, a body that explains your main points, and a conclusion to wrap up your thoughts. Keep in mind that some discussion boards may require longer responses depending on the assignment. Refer to the following example provided below for guidance on structure and content:

Your Name:

Instructor:

Course:

Date:

Title

In response to the prompt, I believe that (insert your main idea or perspective). This topic is significant because (explain why it matters). One key aspect to consider is (insert first main point). For example, (provide an example or evidence). Granted, (insert second main point) is important because_____. This can be seen in (provide another example or evidence). That said, (insert third main point) adds another layer by_____. This is illustrated by (provide an example). In conclusion, (summarize your main argument or perspective). I encourage further discussion on this topic because (insert a thought-provoking statement).

Discussion Board Outlines and Replies

Note: A discussion board reply typically includes four parts: acknowledgment of the original post, agreement or disagreement with reasoning, additional insights or examples, and encouragement for continued conversation. While replies are often around 250–300 words, be sure to follow any specific instructions from your instructor. The following is an example of a basic discussion board reply within the typical 250–300 word range:

_____, (Name of classmate you are responding to)

    I appreciate your insights on (mention a specific point from their post). I agree/disagree with your perspective (insert point). This resonates/does not resonate with me because_____. While I see your point about (insert point), I have a different/similar view. I believe that_____. To build on your ideas, I'd like to add that (insert additional thoughts or examples). Have you considered (a question)? This could provide further insight into_____. I look forward to hearing more about your thoughts _____..

CHAPTER THREE

BASIC OUTLINE

Introduction:

The basic outline serves as the foundation of any well-written assignment. It is a tool for organizing your thoughts, ensuring that your writing is clear, logical, and coherent. In this chapter, we will discuss how to construct a simple yet effective outline, which can be applied to a wide variety of writing tasks. Whether you're preparing for a research paper, an essay, or a report, the basic outline structure will help you stay on track and maintain a focus on the main ideas. See the examples for a clear understanding of how to apply this method to your own work.

Your Name:

Instructor:

Course:

Date:

BASIC OUTLINE

Introduction

1. _____ once stated, "_____."
2. In this essay, I will _____.
3. The topic of _____ is important because_____.
4. **Thesis Statement:** In this essay, I will discuss that _____.

Body Paragraph 1

1. **Topic Sentence A:** The first point I want to make is_____.
2. For example, research shows that_____.
3. This means that _____.
4. Overall, this point demonstrates that _____.

Body Paragraph 2

1. **Topic Sentence B:** Another important point is _____.
2. For instance, many experts believe that _____.
3. This indicates that _____.
4. Although, this evidence supports the idea that _____.

Body Paragraph 3

1. **Topic Sentence C:** Lastly, I will discuss _____.
2. A relevant case is _____.
3. This suggests that _____.
4. Thus, this final point reinforces the argument that_____.

Conclusion

1. Restate your thesis
2. Restate Topic Sentence A
3. Restate Topic Sentence B
4. Restate Topic Sentence C
5. **Final thought:** Ultimately, it is important to consider_____.

CHAPTER FOUR

RHETORICAL ANALYSIS OUTLINE

Introduction:

Rhetorical analysis is a method of critically examining how an author uses language and structure to persuade or inform their audience. In this chapter, we will explore how to create an outline for a rhetorical analysis essay. The focus will be on identifying the key elements of rhetorical situations: the author, audience, purpose, and context, as well as examining the strategies the author uses to achieve their goals. We will break down the process of organizing your analysis logically and effectively. Be sure to review the examples provided to guide your approach to writing a thorough rhetorical analysis.

Your Name:

Instructor:

Course:

Date:

RHETORICAL ANALYSIS OUTLINE

Introduction

1. _____ once stated, "_____."
2. This quote illustrates _____.
3. (author's first and last name, type of text, and title of work) argues that_____.
4. The author's choice of _____ (mention a rhetorical strategy, such as ethos, pathos, logos, or specific stylistic devices) serves to _____ (explain the effect of this strategy on the audience).
5. Additionally, the use of _____ (another rhetorical strategy) enhances the overall argument by _____ (explain how this strategy contributes to the author's message).
6. Through these rhetorical choices, the author aims to _____ (state the author's primary purpose or goal).
7. **Thesis:** (author's last name) effectively convinces his/her audience that _____ through the use of _____ and _____, paired with _____.

Body Paragraph 1: Rhetorical Strategy 1

1. **Topic Sentence A:** The text employs a number of important rhetorical devices, such as _____, which effectively encourages a strong logos appeal to logic.
2. This is supported when the author first _____, then_____, and finally _____.
3. For instance, the author states that_____.
4. This use of _____effectively _____ explains to the readers because _____.

5. Overall, this strategy helps to strengthen the author's argument by_____.

Body Paragraph 2: Rhetorical Strategy 2

1. **Topic Sentence B:** Well defended pathos-appeal to emotion is on of (author's last name) most efficient strategies of demonstrating _____.
2. A specific example can be found when the author writes _____.
3. This example not only exhibits_____, but also signifies_____.
4. This technique appeals to emotion by _____.
5. This is revealed when the author _____, then _____, and lastly_____.
6. Thus, this strategy enhances the author's ability to persuade the audience by _____.

Body Paragraph 3: Rhetorical Strategy 3

1. **Topic Sentence C:** Last but not least, the author also employs ethos, or appeal to ethics, which is one of the most effective ways to indicate _____.
2. This assertion is backed with the following three statements within the text: _____, _____, and _____.
3. In one part of the text, the author highlights_____.
4. This approach is effective because it emphasizes_____.
5. In summary, this strategy is crucial for _____ because _____.

Conclusion

1. Restate your thesis
2. Restate Topic Sentence A
3. Restate Topic Sentence B
4. Restate Topic Sentence C
5. **Final thought:** Ultimately, understanding these strategies helps us appreciate
_____.

CHAPTER FIVE

LITERARY ANALYSIS OUTLINE

Introduction:

Literary analysis requires you to examine a piece of literature closely, considering its themes, characters, structure, and language. Creating an outline for a literary analysis essay is essential to ensure that your arguments are organized and presented clearly. This chapter will walk you through the key components of a literary analysis outline, helping you break down a piece of literature in a systematic and thoughtful way. You'll learn how to develop a strong thesis and structure your paper around supporting evidence. Check the examples provided for further clarification on how to approach this type of analysis.

Your Name:

Instructor:

Course:

Date:

LITERARY ANALYSIS OUTLINE

Introduction

1. _____ once stated, "_____."
2. This quote illustrates _____.
3. One compelling example of this is found in _____ (title of the literary work) by _____ (author's name), where _____ (briefly describe the central theme or conflict).
4. Through the use of _____ (mention a literary device or technique, such as symbolism, imagery, or character development), the author explores _____ (explain the significance or theme revealed by this device).
5. Additionally, the author employs _____ (another literary device) to _____ (explain its effect on the narrative or characters).
6. **Thesis:** (author's last name) use of _____ (first device or technique) and _____ (second device or technique) demonstrates that _____ (state the main argument or insight about the work) and displays the theme of _____.

Body Paragraph 1: Literary Element 1

1. **Topic Sentence A:** One key literary element in the work is_____.
2. For instance, the author uses "_____" (quote or specific example) to illustrate_____.
3. This element is significant because it reveals _____.
4. Therefore, the use of _____deepens the reader's understanding of _____.

Body Paragraph 2: Literary Element 2

1. **Topic Sentence B:** Another important element is _____.
2. A notable example can be found when the author describes _____.
3. This choice of _____ (literary device) highlights_____(theme) by_____.
4. Hence, this element enhances the overall impact of the work by_____.

Body Paragraph 3: Literary Element 3

1. **Topic Sentence C:** Finally, the author also employs _____.
2. For example, _____(quote or situation) serves to _____.
3. This technique is effective because it _____.
4. In summary, this literary element plays a crucial role in conveying _____.

Conclusion

1. Restate your thesis
2. Restate Topic Sentence A
3. Restate Topic Sentence B
4. Restate Topic Sentence C
5. Ultimately, this exploration of the text helps us appreciate the depth of _____ (theme or message) in literature.

CHAPTER SIX
ARGUMENTATIVE OUTLINE

Introduction:

In argumentative writing, your goal is to present a compelling case on a particular issue, backed by evidence and logical reasoning. A well-organized argumentative outline helps you structure your essay in a way that clearly presents your argument and supports it with facts, statistics, or expert opinions. In this chapter, we will discuss how to build an argumentative outline, from introducing your topic to presenting your claims and counterarguments. The examples included will demonstrate how to build a strong argument that engages readers and effectively conveys your position.

ARGUMENTATIVE OUTLINE

Introduction

1. _____ once stated, "_____."
2. This quote illustrates _____.
3. In contemporary society, _____ (introduce the broader topic or issue that is relevant and engaging).
4. One significant aspect of this issue is _____ (narrow down to a specific argument or perspective).
5. Many argue that _____ (present a common viewpoint or counterargument), but this perspective overlooks _____ (briefly state a flaw or limitation in that viewpoint).
6. It is crucial to recognize that _____ (state your main argument or position clearly).
7. **Thesis:** Despite (opposing view)_____, (your position)_____ is the best solution because_____(reason 1), _____ (reason 2), and _____ (reason 3).

Body Paragraph 1: Argument 1

1. **Topic Sentence A:** One strong reason supporting my argument is _____.
2. For example, _____(provide a statistic, quote, or example).
3. This shows that _____.
4. Therefore, this evidence strengthens the case for _____.

Body Paragraph 2: Argument 2

1. **Topic Sentence B:** Another reason to consider is _____.
2. In addition, _____ (provide another piece of evidence).
3. This indicates that _____.
4. Thus, this point further supports the argument that _____.

Body Paragraph 3: Counterargument

1. Topic Sentence C: Some might argue that _____.
2. For instance, _____.
3. However, this view is flawed because _____.
4. This demonstrates that _____(explain why your argument is stronger).

Conclusion

1. Restate your thesis
2. Restate Topic Sentence A
3. Restate Topic Sentence B
4. Restate Topic Sentence C
5. Ultimately, addressing _____ is crucial because it affects _____.

CHAPTER SEVEN

COMPARISON/CONTRAST OUTLINE

Introduction:

Comparison and contrast essays are designed to explore the similarities and differences between two or more subjects. Organizing your essay with a clear outline ensures that you compare and contrast the elements in a logical and structured manner. This chapter will teach you how to create a comparison/contrast outline, guiding you through the process of organizing your subjects in a way that highlights both their similarities and differences. By examining the provided examples, you will gain a better understanding of how to approach and organize your own comparison/contrast essays.

Your Name:

Instructor:

Course:

Date:

COMPARISON/CONTRAST OUTLINE

Introduction

1. _____ once stated, "_____."
2. This quote illustrates _____.
3. In literature, as well as in life, comparisons between subjects can reveal deeper insights into their characteristics and themes.
4. A compelling example of this is found in _____ (mention the first subject, text, or concept) and _____ (mention the second subject, text, or concept), both of which address _____ (briefly describe the common theme or topic).
5. While _____ (state a key similarity between the two subjects), there are also significant differences, such as _____ (mention a key difference).
6. Understanding these similarities and differences is essential to grasp _____ (state the significance of your comparison or contrast).
7. **Thesis:** By examining _____ (list the specific aspects you will compare or contrast), it becomes clear that _____ (conclude with the overarching insight or conclusion).

Body Paragraph 1: Similarities

1. **Topic Sentence A:** Both (Subject A) and (Subject B) share several similarities.
2. Firstly, they both _____.
3. For example, _____.
4. This similarity shows that _____.
5. Therefore, _____.

Body Paragraph 2: Differences

1. **Topic Sentence B:** Despite their similarities, there are notable differences between (Subject A) and (Subject B).
2. One key difference is _____.
3. For instance, _____.
4. Consequently this difference highlights _____.

Body Paragraph 3: Additional Comparison

1. **Topic Sentence C:** Another aspect to consider is _____.
2. While (Subject A) tends to _____, (Subject B) _____.
3. This is evident when _____.
4. This contrast shows how _____.

Conclusion

1. Restate your thesis
2. Restate Topic Sentence A
3. Restate Topic Sentence B
4. Restate Topic Sentence C
5. In the end, understanding these comparisons helps us appreciate _____ in a broader context.

CHAPTER EIGHT

PERSONAL NARRATIVE OUTLINE

Introduction:

Personal narratives are stories that allow you to share your own experiences in a reflective and engaging manner. Crafting an outline for a personal narrative helps you structure your story so that it unfolds in a clear and compelling way. In this chapter, we will discuss how to develop a personal narrative outline, focusing on the introduction, body, and conclusion, while ensuring that your story is engaging and reflects on its meaning. Review the examples included to see how to create a personal narrative that effectively communicates your experiences and their significance.

Your Name:

Instructor:

Course:

Date:

PERSONAL NARRATIVE OUTLINE

Introduction

1. _____ once stated, "_____."
2. This quote illustrates _____.
3. Personal narratives offer a powerful way to share individual experiences and insights that shape who we are.
4. One pivotal moment in my life occurred when _____ (briefly describe the event or experience that will be discussed).
5. This experience taught me _____ (state the lesson or insight gained from the experience), which has had a lasting impact on my perspective.
6. Reflecting on this moment allows me to understand _____ (explain the broader significance or themes related to your experience).
7. **Thesis:** By recounting this experience, I hope to convey _____ (conclude with what you want readers to take away from your narrative).

Body Paragraph 1: Setting the Scene

1. **Topic Sentence A:** To understand my story, it's important to know about _____.
2. The atmosphere was _____ (describe the place, sounds, and sights).
3. I felt _____ because_____.

Body Paragraph 2: The Climax

1. **Topic Sentence B:** The turning point of my story came when _____.
2. I vividly remember _____.

3. At that moment, I felt _____.

Body Paragraph 3: Reflection and Growth

1. **Topic Sentence C:** After that experience, I realized that _____.
2. This taught me the importance of _____.
3. I started to see things differently, such as _____.

Conclusion

1. In conclusion, that day taught me that _____.
2. Looking back, I understand how this experience shaped who I am today because of_____.
3. Ultimately, it reminded me of the power of _____.

CHAPTER NINE

FORMAL RESEARCH PAPER OUTLINE

Introduction:

A formal research paper is a comprehensive project that requires a deep dive into a specific topic, often involving extensive research and analysis. The formal research paper outline provides a roadmap for your research, guiding you from your introduction to your conclusion, with clearly defined sections for your argument, methodology, results, and analysis. This chapter will help you create a detailed and organized outline for a formal research paper. By reviewing the examples, you'll understand how to structure your research paper to present your findings in a clear and scholarly manner.

Your Name:

Instructor:

Course:

Date:

FORMAL RESEARCH PAPER OUTLINE

Introduction

1. Fact, question, or statistic about your topic.
2. Define your topic and provide a brief history of it.
3. The issue of _____ has recently grown in importance.
4. Until now, little importance has been given to _____.
5. In order to understand this issue, it is important to examine _____.
6. How would this be different if _____?
7. This study builds on _____ and contributes to _____.
8. The evidence I use to support _____ is _____.
9. **Thesis Statement:** It is widely known that _____, but not many people realize _____.

Body Paragraphs

Paragraph A Topic Sentence:

1. A major part in understanding_____ is _____.
2. It has been suggested that_____ (Author's Last Name page number).
3. According to _____ (page number) _____.
   Author's Last Name

4. Several studies have revealed _____ (Author's Last Name page number).
5. This evidence shows that _____.
6. Although, _____.

Paragraph B Topic Sentence:

1. Another important factor to consider is _____.
2. Data from several studies have identified _____ (Author's Last Name page number).
3. It is thought that _____.
4. This view is supported by _____ (page number), who states_____.

Author's Last Name

5. This indicates that _____.
6. In addition to the previous points, _____.

Paragraph C Topic Sentence:

1. Further consideration involves_____.
2. A considerable amount of literature has been published on _____.
3. However, there has been relatively little literature published on _____.
4. The research to date has tended to focus on _____ (Author's Last Name page number).
5. This illustrates that _____.
6. On the other hand, _____.

Paragraph D Topic Sentence:

1. Equally important is the fact that _____.
2. It has been demonstrated that _____ (Author's Last Name page number).
3. Research shows that _____ (Author's Last Name page number).
4. This reinforces the idea that _____.
5. The key takeaways are _____.
6. With this in mind, _____.

Paragraph E Topic Sentence:

1. Another key factor to consider is _____.
2. Numerous studies have mentioned that _____.
3. One important aspect of _____ is _____.
4. Studies have found that _____ (Author's Last Name page number).
5. This finding suggests that _____.
6. Therefore, _____.

Paragraph F Topic Sentence:

1. Lastly, it is crucial to acknowledge_____.
2. It has been conclusively shown that _____ (Author's Last Name page number).
3. This further supports _____.
4. It's possible that _____.
5. This evidence makes it clear that _____.
6. In closing, _____.

Conclusion

1. **Restate Thesis**
2. Restate **Paragraph A Topic Sentence**
3. Restate **Paragraph B Topic Sentence**
4. Restate **Paragraph C Topic Sentence**
5. Restate **Paragraph D Topic Sentence**
6. Restate **Paragraph E Topic Sentence**
7. Restate **Paragraph F Topic Sentence**
8. Given these findings, it is clear that further research into _____ is necessary.

In-Text Citation Guidelines (MLA):

- For a book: *(Author's Last Name, page number)*
- For an article: *(Author's Last Name, page number)*
- For a website: *(Author's Last Name)* (if no page number is available).

Reference Page/Works Cited Setup for Various Sources (MLA):

1. Books

Format:
Author's Last Name, First Name. *Title of Book*. Publisher, Year of Publication.

Example:
Anderson, Emily. *Digital Communication and Society*. HarperCollins, 2020.

2. Articles (Journal or Magazine)

Format:
Author's Last Name, First Name. "Title of Article." *Title of Journal or Magazine*, vol. number, no. number, Year, pages.

Example:
Johnson, Sarah. "The Impact of Digital Communication on Mental Health." *Journal of Modern Media*, vol. 22, no. 3, 2021, pp. 100-115.

3. Journals (Online Databases like JSTOR or Google Scholar)

Format:
Author's Last Name, First Name. "Title of Article." *Title of Journal*, vol. number, no. number, Year, pp. pages. *Name of Database*, URL.

Example:
Brown, Lisa. "Exploring Digital Interaction in Education." *Journal of Digital Learning*, vol. 12, no. 4, 2022, pp. 45-56. *JSTOR*, www.jstor.org/stable/1234567.

4. Websites

Format:
Author's Last Name, First Name. "Title of Webpage or Article." *Title of Website*, Publisher (if available), Date of Publication, URL.

Example:
Miller, John. "Managing Screen Time for Better Mental Health." *HealthToday*, 25 May 2023, www.healthtoday.com/mental-health/screen-time.

In-Text Citation Guidelines (APA):

- **For a book**: (Author's Last Name, Year, p. Page Number)
- **For an article**: (Author's Last Name, Year, p. Page Number)
- **For a website**: (Author's Last Name, Year) (if no page number is available).

Reference Page/Works Cited Setup for Various Sources (APA):

1. Books

Format:
Author's Last Name, First Initial. (Year). *Title of book*. Publisher.
Example:
Anderson, E. (2020). *Digital communication and society*. HarperCollins.

2. Articles (Journal or Magazine)

Format:
Author's Last Name, First Initial. (Year). Title of article. *Title of Journal or Magazine*, *Volume*(Issue), pages.

Example:
Johnson, S. (2021). The impact of digital communication on mental health. *Journal of Modern Media*, *22*(3), 100–115.

3. Journals (Online Databases like JSTOR or Google Scholar)

Format:
Author's Last Name, First Initial. (Year). Title of article. *Title of Journal, Volume*(Issue), pages. *Name of Database*, URL

Example:
Brown, L. (2022). Exploring digital interaction in education. *Journal of Digital Learning, 12*(4), 45–56. JSTOR, https://www.jstor.org/stable/1234567.

4. Websites

Format:
Author's Last Name, First Initial. (Year, Month Day). Title of webpage or article. *Title of Website*. URL

Example:
Miller, J. (2023, May 25). Managing screen time for better mental health. *HealthToday*. https://www.healthtoday.com/mental-health/screen-time

CHAPTER 10

ANNOTATED BIBLIOGRAPHY

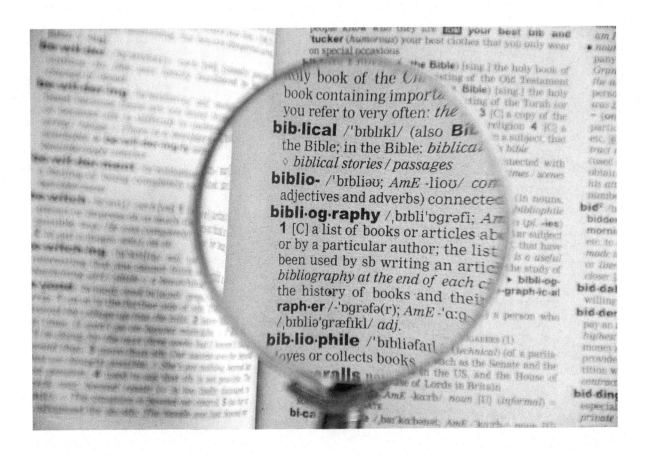

Introduction:

An annotated bibliography is a valuable tool for organizing and analyzing research sources. It combines citations with concise summaries and evaluations of each source, helping you assess their relevance and reliability for your research. This chapter will guide you through the process of creating an annotated bibliography, focusing on proper citation formatting and the key elements of annotation: summarizing, assessing, and reflecting on each source. By reviewing the examples included, you will gain a clear understanding of how to construct an effective annotated bibliography to support your academic or professional research endeavors.

Your Name:

Instructor:

Course:

Date:

ANNOTATED BIBLIOGRAPHY OUTLINE

Introduction: Paragraph 1

1. Research topic question.
2. The rationale behind the research topic selection_____.
3. The types of sources included_____.
4. The process used to locate the sources_____.
5. Ethical implications (risk) _____.
6. The importance of further research_____.
7. **Thesis Statement** (Solution to the problem…declarative statement).

Body Paragraph 2

1st Citation_____.
1. In this article, (author's last name) reviews_____.
2. The main ideas expressed are_____.
3. The author provides a strong theoretical_____.
4. This article is useful for the research topic _____.

Body Paragraph 3

1st Citation_____.
1. This article examines_____.
2. Support for these claims is documented_____.
3. The writing style considers a range of audiences_____.
4. The information if from a reliable source because _____.

Body Paragraph 4

1st Citation_____.
1. The author describes_____.
2. _____ (author's last name) has conducted a thorough investigation of _____.
3. Theories are supported by well-known researchers in this field, such as_____.
4. It is relevant to the thesis because _____.

Body Paragraph 5

1st Citation_____.
1. The author's purpose is to challenge_____.
2. The author's research focuses on_____.
3. There is a lack of supporting evidence_____.
4. In particular, this article will assist _____.

Conclusion: Paragraph 6

1. Restate Thesis Statement
2. Restate 1st Sentence in Paragraph 2
3. Restate 1st Sentence in Paragraph 3
4. Restate 1st Sentence in Paragraph 4
5. Restate 1st Setence in Paragraph 5
6. Closing thoughts

Printed in the United States
by Baker & Taylor Publisher Services

Dr. Puntwida L. Trezvant is an accomplished author and educator with a passion for empowering students to excel in writing. With over 20 years of experience in both high school and college-level teaching, she has dedicated her career to guiding students through the challenges of writing and learning. She is the author of five books, including this comprehensive textbook and study guide designed to help English students overcome writing difficulties.

Dr. Puntwida L. Trezvant is the founder of several educational businesses, with a strong commitment to improving educational outcomes across various disciplines. Her academic achievements are vast and include two Associate's Degrees, a Bachelor of Arts in Psychology, Education, and Sociology from Wichita State University, and two Master's Degrees—one in Education from Belhaven University and one in Human Sciences with a focus on Sociology and Leadership from Our Lady of the Lake University. She also holds Doctoral Executive Certificates in Higher Education Administration and Law and Policy from Liberty University, and is currently completing her third Master's in Interdisciplinary Studies with an emphasis on English and Leadership.

Dr. Puntwida L. Trezvant currently serves as a College Professor, teaching a variety of subjects, including English, Sociology, Teacher Education, and Law, while continuing to share her expertise with students and educators alike. Her dedication to education, combined with her personal commitment to helping students succeed, makes her a respected figure in the academic community.

In addition to her teaching career, Dr. Puntwida L. Trezvant is a proud mother of one adult daughter and a devoted "grandmother" to her Yorkie granddog. Throughout her career, she has earned numerous awards and certificates in education, business, and law.

ISBN 979-8-3694-4187-9

ibris

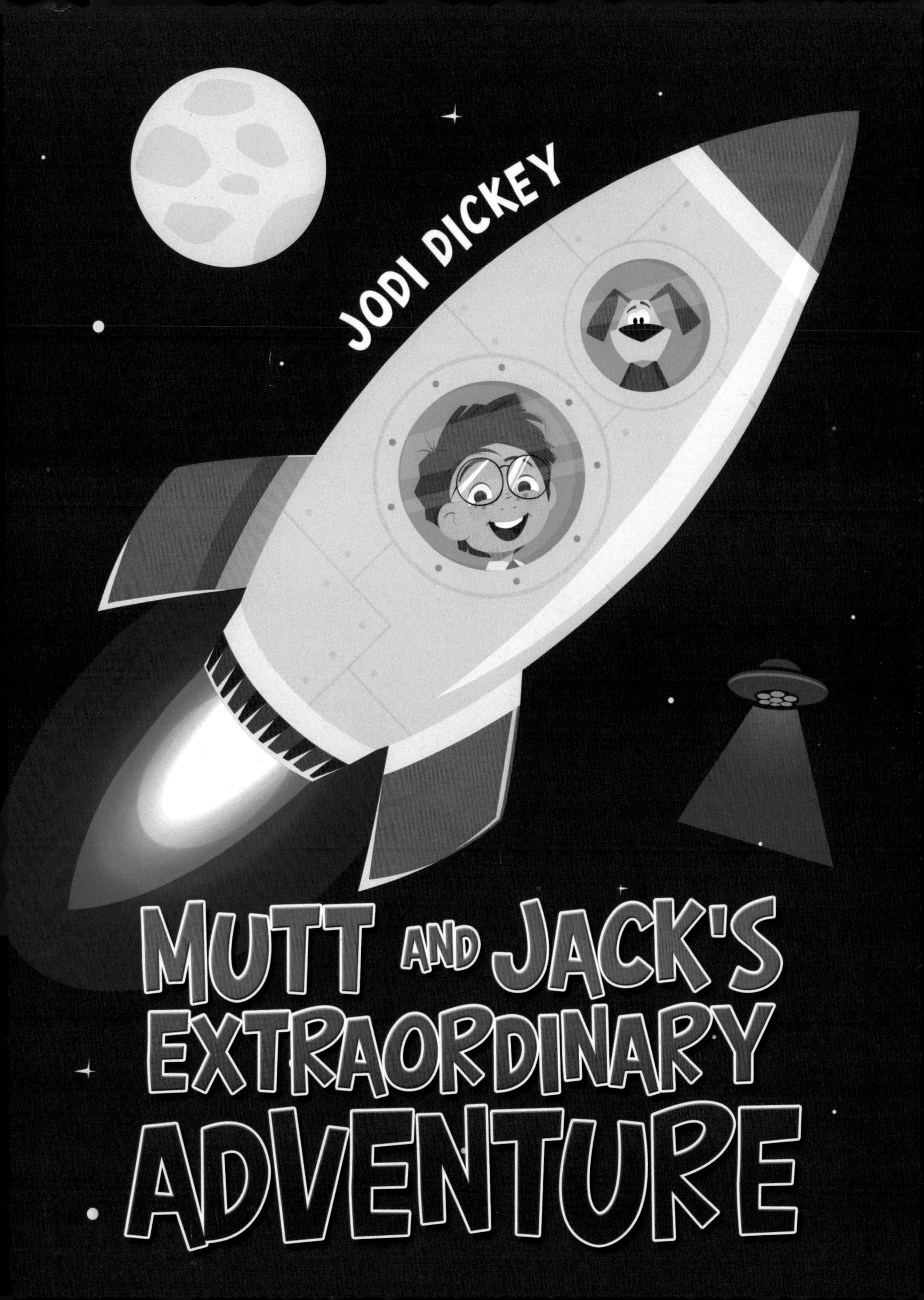
JODI DICKEY
MUTT AND JACK'S
EXTRAORDINARY
ADVENTURE